T0114665

Heartdrops

A Love Story In Poems

Jose M Yrizarry

authorHOUSE

AuthorHouse™
1663 Liberty Drive
Bloomington, IN 47403
www.authorhouse.com
Phone: 833-262-8899

Published by AuthorHouse   10/23/2023

ISBN: 979-8-8230-1661-2 (sc)
ISBN: 979-8-8230-1662-9 (e)

Library of Congress Control Number: 2023920865

Print information available on the last page.

Any people depicted in stock imagery provided by Getty Images are models, and such images are being used for illustrative purposes only. Certain stock imagery © Getty Images.

This book is printed on acid-free paper.

About the Author

JOSE YRIZARRY: Born in Brooklyn, N.Y. and influenced by his studies in Sociology and Deviant Behavior at John Jay College, Jose dedicated himself as a history/English teacher and crisis counselor working with "At Risk Youth." He went on to developing and implementing programs in community outreach, dropout prevention, and alternatives to incarceration for organizations like Outward Bound, Planned Parenthood, The National Congress for Neighborhood Woman, and El Puente After School Center. He is a published author, an established performing poet, and former editor/writer for The New Tomorrow, a monthly newspaper published on the lower east side of Manhattan/NYC. Recently joining another community-based publication, "The Buffalo Latino Village", he established a monthly column: "Community Outreach and Empowerment." His writing can also be found in his blog "Urban Predators Speak Out" and to appreciate his unique and amazing poetic works visit his video collection on YouTube.

<u>Available for live performances</u>

347 – 865 – 3160
<u>Joepy4@yahoo.com</u>

Sample his writing on blogspot
<u>https://2bspoken.blogspot.com/</u>

Sample his video collection on You Tube
<u>https://www.youtube.com/@joseyrizarrythepoeticurban8475/videos</u>

Jose Yrizarry – The Urban Predator

Dedicated to my mother, Julia Yrizarry, and the many wonderful women, buddies like Ruth and Sandra, that have crossed and influenced my path

Moms Legacy Decreed

She came to be, learned the way, stayed the course, and grew
Mentally - physically and spiritually
A faithful servant of her lord …
A faithful daughter, sister, wife, mom, aunt, and friend
to all that crossed her path without regrets.
No doubt came rain on her parade - came thunder to test her faith
and unexpected lightning strikes to break some dreams
she silently, valiantly had to hold and persevere
For sake of three God gave into her hands
to lead provide protect and teach …
A task she carried out in and with both words and deeds
while on secret bended knees she faced daybreak
while others simply went to sleep.
Knowing her strength came from up above
she struggled, sacrificed, and grew
always training, strengthening, and maintaining …
wasting not time or energy – talents or words.
Setting examples everyday hour and minute
She was proud but humble, caring but firm
She worked hard and like a good steward
She penny pinched to make ends meet
Thus, her three were never left in neither want or need
And yet through it all made time she did
to laugh and play each and every day.
Yes! She stayed the course, ran the race three generations long
and fought the fight from dawn to dusk
while through it all kept her tears tween her and God.
Thus now, her covenant with him made complete
Does come her final breath and just reward!
She has not died but gone to be made one with her lord.
So don't stand by her grave and weep
for now she's been set free - unbound to carry on …
upon a thousand winds that blow –
upon the diamonds glint on snow –
upon the sunlight shine on ripened grain –
she's the gentle autumn rain - and In the morning hush
she's the swift uplifting rush of quiet birds in circle flight
and the soft stars that shine at night so bright.
So do not stand at her grave and weep for she's not there
but buried ever deep inside every heart she came to touch
*** A psalm from Son to Mom (6/2022) ***

Introduction

~~~~~~~~~~~~~~~~~~~~~~~~~~~~~~~~~~~~~~~

<u>Love Reasons</u>

Love reasons what heart and mind cannot …
Regardless of where it goes or where it's from
Ringing true for all … Love reasons!
A condition springing from the past
To test
Both present and future stance
With thunder sparking rain clouds
In both heart and mind.
For how long or why, no one knows.
So what's wrong?
If loves still not gone! – Still not Time to Move on!
Cause love still reasons
What heart and mind can not

Contents

My Mind

~~~~~~~~~~~~~~~~~~~~~~~~~~~~~~~~~~~~~~~

It blows my mind each and every time
I see you passing by
Your eyes, your smile and swaying stride
makes me want to say please stay …
Lets play a game in life far from strife and fight
Lets just simply blow each others mind
Each and every time.
Within its game of truth and dare
Love's gates are made open wide to explore
where you stand and who you really are
in both heart and mind

(So tell me who you are) >>>

Who are you?

Who are you?
Are you the east wind that brings the breeze and shine of dawn
Or
The westward draft that brings the setting sun and chill of night
Who are you?
Are you the sign of things that might but never come to pass
Or
The sign of things that are and only need the gardener's hand
Who are you?
Are you the southern front that blossoms things that come in time
Or
The northern blast that brittles down the deepest warmest thoughts
Cause
I'm still not caught in past fears and doubts,
I'm bath beads, bubbles, and wine by candlelight,
I'm that dinner plate beneath moonlight and
That noonday toast when the sun rides high and bright.
I'm that touch that brings to light the depths behind your eyes
And beckons you to smile.
I'm that breath behind your ear
to spring from you an inner song
And that embrace which says
Within these arms no harm or wrong draws near.
I'm that which braves the ether of your soul
If indeed therein lurks a seed to find,
If indeed a dream in you does still resides.
I am - if indeed - you are!
And if per chance you're not
Let your blade be swift and true.
But never shall this heart be stayed
Or this soul be swayed
By the chains of dismay to stay away.
With both heart and soul in me, forever shall we steer
Toward the goal that waits for those who dare mistake.
So tell me who you are and where you stand
… The rest I'll leave to fate …

(Because I am intrigued) >>>

Intrigued

~~~~~~~~~~~~~~~~~~~~~~~~~~~~~~~~~~~~~~

Sitting here intrigued
By what just might t'ween you and me,
By what with pen in hand we'd find
To place on canvas sheets no longer bare.

How sweet the thought of next wine sought
With you right here, then caught,
Our thoughts In wild exchange
If only we would dare to seek
What might unfold to make complete
This sudden moment of intrigue
With next grapes squeezed and shared.

Indeed we'd climb new heights
With passions freed to quench all else
Where burst away past hurts
And set ablaze tomorrows dawn.

How vast the thoughts now shared within our stare
Suffice to touch and dissipate despair …
Where then Your hair I'd long to brush,
Your frame I'd long to touch,
Your scent I'd long to breathe.

And though now gone I know not where
A kindred soul in you I found …
A thing to churn with burning yearn
All because we dared our stare.

And so in hope you'd choose
To let me in and give intrigue it's due,
To bed in wait I turn
Where then there dared to be compared
What treasured moments shared could come,
What secrets might unfold
Like wind more so like ocean waves
Were you to press your lips on mine
To climb the distant heights with me,
To find so full of time to burn with yearn …
This moment of intrigue

(where then I'd be consumed) >>>

3

Consumed

Consumed by fragrant candlelight and silent evening still
Where claws of inner thought dig deep,
So deep beyond both flesh and bone
To where just past the pulse of heart
The sense of soul does wait
A wordless feel that longs the touch
that never seems to come from human hand.

Consumed by timeless claws that dig so deep,
So long beyond where once thought could
By human force be persevered
And yet no doubt …
Beyond the pain of tear
You're there.

Longing for what cannot be then explained
Much less dared or shared
And yet you know – you know you're there!
You know, somewhere beyond - you are!

Consumed in stare so strong
You fear to even blink.
And so you drink and drink love's cup
As if perhaps you might collapse,
As if be then consumed
By an abyss now here …
Awakened and fulfilled …
All your wants and needs
Consumed?

But where might you then be?
Who might you then be?
What might have you become?
Consumed beyond all human sense?
Then whose magic touch did hold the key?
And whose embrace did set you free
When suddenly you opened up your eyes to see?

Can you feel the tug of war from strings deep down within?
Can you hear the strum of drums deep therein?
Can you brave the setting sun of all your known
To now by tomorrows breath be then
Consumed by love?

(then presume you have prevailed) >>>

Presume You Have Prevailed

~~~~~~~~~~~~~~~~~~~~~

Let not presume
A moment here or there worth its weight in wait.
Let not the thongs embrace enchant,
Nor whip of tongue confuse the loins.
Let not the brush of lips upon the brow
Erase all thought …
Nor touch upon the breast consume the heart in flames.
Let glitter not detain the eye,
Nor harp prevail to dull the ear.
For many here to flesh do fall
And never leave its drinking well.

Let not presume
A moment here or there worth its weight in wait;
When standing at that narrow gate,
Where all to loose – where all to gain,
It beckons one that call …
That sound that stirs ones all for all
And then … suddenly …
Into Gods open arms … One Leaps

One Leaps to where
One's deeper self unveiled …
Its blinding glow a never ending flow.
Ones leap to find all sense prevails
To laugh, to cry, to live and die in both woe and awe
Where then one can presume
Indeed you have prevailed
With but one leap … indeed …
love has once again prevailed

(but to what avail) >>>

To what Avail

To what avail have you prevailed?
To stalk and stalk again
As if some inner mongrel been unleashed,
As if no other choice be left than feast?
Are you not more than beast?
Then for shame you have prevailed
And to shame be dragged all you've come to yield

For no more than thief shall you be called
On love's ever lasting scrolls
And as in its blood shall you be soaked,
In its ashes, so to, shall you be cloaked.
For never shall love's honor tap your door
Nor its glory light your path.

For to what avail have you prevailed?
More so for what have you been spared
But to shine with the evening stars
And to glow with the morning rise.
To burrow the valley with your seeds
And climb the heights with your greatest deeds.
For this – beneath love's banner
Let your soul prevail

(by fragrant candlelight and silent evening still) >>>

Silent Still

From silent still within
Reach out to touch beyond
The norm of sight, smell, and sound.

To sense
That which is divine
That which binds
All that is with was and will
On one eternal thread
And so

Transcend the Matrix hype of common here and now

To span the flashing splash of space and time
Where then .. In bliss
In eye to eye with all
The press of freedoms lips upon our brow

To kiss away the tears of was
To kiss away the fear of might
To kiss in present light
The awe that will ascend
When unity of all is found

Where then
In silent still not void
We Are

(And thus suppose it not a spell) >>>

Suppose

Suppose a flower has outgrown
its pot of years now gone by.
Suppose on fields a new,
beneath new rays of sun,
new leaves it does begin to sprout
where then waiting to embrace …

A breeze of southern warmth
suffice to chase away
the northern frost
that often tends to keep
So many hearts
from sensing throbs still yet to come …

Like ocean waves upon some tropic shore
where then
as if brought forth by mystic hands of grace
Not only foot prints in the sand
but a humming sound of bees within our heads as well
As if … As if it were a spell …

Suffice to cause
That flower now to bloom a new.

And so it is
when kindred spirits cross
to change what might seem strange to most …
When strangers bloom and bond as friends …
Suppose it not a Spell

(suppose it all a touched twilight moment) >>>

A Touched Twilight

~~~~~~~~~~~~~~~~~~~~~~~~~~~

One look, that's all it took
And suddenly so much
I wanted to touch, hold, and squeeze
Till my desires deep,
Made well appeased
By your sudden scent and feel unbound

And so to my dismay
Encased within a desire to chase and taste,
An appeal longing to be made …
Forbidden fruit
Dangled just beyond my sight

Not fun – Not fun!
The sun whose heated rays
Once raced to place upon my brow
A bead of sweat while setting up a tone
Among the many bells within my head that rung.
Let not this night find you in flight.
Find me in struggle and in fight
With we made separate and alone

Just come home.
Come home with me and see
This feel set free and real
Where tomorrow,
Beneath new sheets made void
Of sorrow and regret …
We, found and together bound

If you but hear and feel the sounds
Of heart felt moans and groans,
Of dividing stone walls falling to the ground
Where we, free of sorrows and regrets …
Love bound and together found

Just because one look is all it took
For much to touch, hold, and squeeze
When desires deep are found and made so well appeased
Embraced! By loves scent suddenly made unbound
Within a touched twilight

(to then be traced) >>>

Traced

There they were … There we are
Ones eyes like sparkling stars shinning bright,
Ones smile like horizons new before my sight,
Both making the night a thing so right,
Both making desires might an internal fight.
And though now gone,
Out of sight but close in mind,
How warm and kind
They were! We are …
A welcomed sign to lay and close my eyes.
They! We! Both by my side like wings
To brave new heights.
Heights where once again
With pen and pad to write,
These words to complement ones state of mind
These words - a sign!
A sign that says
Let not this be - last time.

For I'd love your hand once more to touch,
Your hair once more to brush,
Your eyes once more to search
While perched once more, we side by side
Where then …
Your sigh from deep inside I'd find,
Where then
Your thoughtful mind unveiled,
Where then
Our heart and soul like fertile fields in wait,
My words like seeds well placed.
Outpoured!
New hopes and dreams to taste …
A pulsing race where chased,
A we in wild embrace,
A we among the clouds then graced
With all that might, could, and should be traced

(because you are) >>>

My Latin Cindered "Ella"

From within the mist of all that was she came…
In and Out of crowds then made no more.
Like a small but shinning shooting star
That streaked across horizons now my own.
To wish my hopes and dreams upon …
She Is!

A trail of flames that burned away my past,
A spark from deep within to chase and taste her fruits
As if tomorrow was no more than just a step
From dark to light free of fright or fight.
And yet I stayed …
I stayed away!

Till now no more than just a weighted prayer within my soul remains
A prayer … A prayer!
That longs to hear her melody begin to fill my ears,
That longs to gaze upon her frame so full of grace and charm,
That's longs to sense her penetrating stare once more.
Once more!

Her name that now escapes the corridor of my thoughts,
Till now no more than just a constant sting within my brain remains.
A string of memories playing hide and seek
Within the leaves of some enchanting tree still full of possibilities
To tease beneath its branches full of chance and breeze,
Like breaths of thoughts still caught but lingering.

Unappeased! This quest that now unlocks my sense to feel once more.
Within her eyes so dark and deep,
So large enough to catch my every thought.
And thus I see … my latin cindered "Ella"
Her rise, a sacrificial smoke to smell and put to rest
The glitter of her slipper pressed to walk right by my side.

Now fading fast into a sky too vast for me to grasp
Too vast! The thought of future chance
Rising in sacrificial puffs of smoke
That latin cindered "Ella" full of hope to cope
Fading fast within the skies of future chance
Now near gone …
The glistening slipper of that Latin Cindered "Ella"
Walking by my side.

(suffice to cause a new pulsing thought) >>>

A Pulsing Thought

I pulse at the thought ...
Your face before my eyes,
Your flesh before my finger touch
And sense desires dance made real
As sweet sweat upon my brow begins to form.

Were you not far but near
Without a sense of doubt or fear
Your hair like piano cords i'd stroke,
Your breast like conga drums i'd press
To fill this present empty space
With breath released in gasps

Oh that you would bring to pass
This thought made real enough to share
Where then compared with things now past,
Where then compared with things still yet to come,
The sum of something new to contemplate
As sweet sweat upon my brow begins to form
Another pulsing thought

(because you are an addictive flame) >>>

An addictive Flame

Your addictive flame has made my day
In ways I have to say
I'm sold, you're bold and laced in gold.

You've scorched my brain so strong
I gots to say Right on! Do bring it on!
Song after song! All night long!

Where then, on dance floors kicking up a storm
Your strands like willow trees swaying in the breeze,
Your limbs like thrashing ocean waves
Full of hopes and dreams that scream …
ITS SHOW TIME!
Here and now with we made one,
With no time to fabricate reasons for blame,
This chance to chase and contemplate what's yet to come.

Where then close and tight in each others arms,
Hearing the ringing of each others lucky charms,
Our thoughts turning into shooting stars
To chart the rhythmic plains of foreplay.

Where then, within life's active deck of cards
A game full of hearts for us to find
Diamond tips carving out a brand-new day,
While swinging clubs and cutting blades of spades
Brings it all to boil - within foreplay
While fanning hot each other's blazing soul …
Songs to proclaim – your addictive flame to carry on

(our love - like an anchor in the storm) .>>>

Anchor in the storm

Always been – always be
An anchor in the storm

Come rain or shine,
Come winds tearing at these walls of mine,
Come heaven's glitter for me to store,
Come hell knocking at the door

Always been – always be
An anchor in the storm

I may come sore,
I may come rotted to the core,
No matter what I be,
Fruits from her I always see dangling from her tree

Cause always been – always be
She – an anchor in the storm

And so because of her I soar
Eagle winged spread wide and far
For after all that's what friends are for …
who can ask for more

Cause always been – always be
An ever-treasured anchor in the storm is she

(something to capture on canvas olive brown) >>>

Canvas Olive Brown

On a canvas olive brown
For all eyes to rest and gaze upon,
Traced and sliced just right
A warm and radiant sun filled smile …
A pair of twinkle star lit eyes
Full of life and so much more …
A pair of proud dark brows
Crowned by amber strands
That rest on shoulders stout and strong
Unblemished and untamed!
A tribal flame is what she is.
And so from a distance - Unnoticed and safe
Through the wind - From here to there,
With a whispered hiss …
And a bliss filled kiss
To rest upon her vibrant Latin soul
Where then to rest my thoughts
On her Canvas Olive Brown

(cause she is indeed a flower) >>>

Velvet Rose

~~~~~~~~~~~~~~~~~~~~~~~~~~~~~~~~

She calls herself an orchid,
A wildflower blooming toward the sun
While I simply call her velvet rose ...
A thing whose pellets captivate both sight and scent,
A thing whose thorns bring but a gentle thought ...
"Give not a pull or tug for sake things not wither into dust"
And so ... Be Slow ...
To see its nature glow – Just be gentle, just be Slow ...
Just please don't let things fade or disappear
Just stick around and watch things grow
From misty memories to present thrills of possibilities.
Cause though she calls herself an orchid
A wildflower blooming toward the sun
I simply call her velvet rose
A suspenseful journey across the ski,
A moment in time where our embrace will tell no lie.
And So
"Give not a pull or tug for sake things not wither as a dream"
Let's simply just be gentle
Just be slow ...
To see our nature glow – simply just Let Go
Let Go – But please don't go.
Just stick around and watch us grow
From thrill of possibilities to profound actualities
Cause while she calls herself an orchid
A wildflower blooming toward the sun
I simply call her velvet rose ...

(as another moment does unfold)

For the moment

For the moment …
You come close, so close and real
You pass through me like music
Rekindling an old, old flame
Still deep, amber hot, and creeping
Round the corridors of my mind where now
… For the moment …
Intrigued by memories still in me
You come close, so close and real
… I feel …
My fields of dreams like refreshed leaves
Beneath a summer noonday rain
Shining, enlightening, and enticing,
Collaborating with my every breath and pulse.
And so – for now
Intrigued by mysteries unveiled
So close and real
I must admit you is my crown
Shining, enlightening, and enticing
For the moment - Another moment
Close and real enough to see and feel

(you a shooting star) >>>

Shooting Star

She comes and goes like a shooting star
Leaving me in a state of no holds barred
… Charred by the heat of how she looks
… Charmed by the music in her voice.

She comes and goes like a shooting star
Leaving me in a state of pounding heart
… As bongo drums humming down in deep
… As maracas shaking goose bumps forming on my skin.

She comes and goes like a shooting star
Leaving me in a state now compromised
… My appetite once more alive
… My whole for her once more does reach
As she streaks across the corridors of my mind
Where now she feels "Right On"
And so "It's On"

So do come on oh shooting star,
Lets make our time last long
Lets make "We" of "You and Me"
And as you streak across my sky
Make my wish for you come true

(cause you're an angel) >>>

Angel

I've heard of angels running all about
And wondered on and off if one like me could count
Just because t'ween slips, flips, and falls
On bended knees - once there - I often pause in prayer
To say at least the stare of faith and trust — my soul has not lost

But never did I hope to find
One such as this to stand before my eyes
Pointing out so subtly - a thing for me to contemplate
A string of pearls still in wait
To chase away the dark despair that tries to cloud my thoughts
T'ween barren lands and threatening storms

And so I thought might I
From wordless heart felt shades of gratitude
Transcribe what I cannot deny
That angels do indeed transcend beyond the mystic realms
To lift and fill the likes of mortal men
Where once again in fearless state
Face the battlefields of fate

And should it come to be - needs for me to feed
For common cause t'ween two now one
My shield of hope I raise
My blade of faith I place before its path and say
May haste find way to always place a blessings plate
Before this feathered angels feet

(A message from above) >>>

A Message From Above

As I struggle to keep the faint frail image
of that first encounter live;
The mystery of her darting eyes,
The peaceful warmth
of those first few words exchanged …
A Dark Abyss
of hopes and dreams I reached
Though her hand in mine still not
Yet she is!
She's there!
Out there somewhere she is …
I sense her presence
And feel her pulse
As if somewhere in her …
A message from the mystic realms
Therein lay for me to find and solve.
Because she throbs like a water drum,
She purrs like a jungle cat
As ripples in my veins do form.
And as a running stream
Forms foam within a pond …
though from dark abyss
Empty handed I return …
I sense her presence
And feel her pulse
As if somewhere in her …
A message from the mystic realms
Therein lay for me to find and solve.
A MESSAGE
A MESSAGE FROM ABOVE

(a message for ones eyes appease) >>>

More than eyes Appease

~~~~~~~~~~~~~~~~~~~~

From distant shores she came
To land before my eyes appease,
To cause within – An inner stir …
A please draw near to test and tease
And thus begins a game of chess.

A rook's left hook around her ribs
A knight's curving squeeze upon her queen-like flanks,
And a bishop's sweep up and down her spine
Just to hold her gaze with a good old cup of wine

Where beneath moon's twilight glow
Present mysteries do unfold
Like endless passing ocean waves
Shifting through the sandy shores within my mind.

Where with thoughts, dreams, and tales exchanged
Treasured footprints forming side by side …
A thing worth calling spice,
A thing worth doing more than once or twice.

All this and more unfolding just because …
Just because our distant paths drew near enough
To stir within desires quest a tease to please
A shinning light to help us seek and find
Much more than just a moment of appease.

(but is she forbidden fruit) >>>

Forbidden Fruit

Out of the twilight
In queen like strut
Her golden fleece appeared
Like a silent evening breeze
to soothe my gaze
so deep, so deep in thoughts
I do dare seek her embrace.
A Forbidden Moments Fruit at best
A moment on a horizon yet to come.
I watched her strutting gate,
I drew her scent with every breath
As if an evening dance among the distant clouds
Would hold the moment for just a little while ...
The mystery still left to find within her eyes,
The subtle stories hid within her gentle smile,
The soothing courage in her touch
As the firmness of her limbs
No doubt – made me begin to sigh
AS I WONDERED WHY ...
I couldn't even say hello

(where now she's but a dream) >>>

Dream

Indeed! How cool to know
Dreams can come to mean much more
Than words dispensed
Throughout life course of daily choirs

How cool to know
It lives and breaths in one like you
So strong, so smooth, so sure and true …
Your moves for me to gaze upon

A matter now to taste and place
Within a long and warm embrace
That just might bring about a purr.
Release! From cold and dark seclude.

It's true!
Your firm yet gentle paws upon my back,
Your waves of flesh to blow my mind,
To catch and fill my thoughts renewed.
… How cool …

Your hips within my claws to squeeze
While pressed my parted lips to trace your spine,
Where then you'd stretch and close your eyes
As brought upon your face another smile to rise

Indeed how cool to know we could
Make walks through parks and ferry rides
A thing well worth exploring more …
Much more than just a dream

This thought …
Having filled my soul anew
Giving chase to thoughts
Streaking across the corridors of my mind
Where then indeed I have to say … Dream On!

(How cool it is) >>>

How Cool

How cool the thought that comes behind your glide
And with a slide right up your spine
There find behind your ear that special place
To let escape a breath that softly says
Let's ride

Let's fly the friendly skies
And find the shine of moon and stars
Within each others eyes
As if made full to chart anew
Our lives

To leave behind the jive of lies
To find the sea so vast and full …
Waves that dare not think to end
But to horizons new then braved;
A dream come true

How cool the thought that comes to find
Behind your glide - my slide;
Made one behind closed eyes and smiles
That would indeed to compromise not arrive
And so! Let's Ride … Our Lives … To Dream

How Cool … the thought
That brings about a dream
Just right to chase across the skies.
With sails made new and full
Indeed I say … how cool

(that thing you just call sport) >>>

24

That Thing You Call just Sport

For changing my frowns into smiles
For pressing me on to agree
Its time for round # 3.
While "Cool Dreams"
Await discoveries to unfold
Here comes a "right on" to "move on"
To that thing you call just sport.
Cause I'm caught in the fun of the thought
Of "How Cool" it would be
To slip into a "Dream"
Just right to help us break free
From all within a gentle breeze.
So do bring it on
From dusk until dawn …
To it all I dare say Right On!
To meet somewhere out there on the streets
And make the heart skip a few beats
To hear passing honking car horns
To place burgers and hot dogs on toasted hot buns
While lip smackin' fries all covered in cheese
Makes sitting by the sea a "Dream" come true
"How Cool" it be
Where beneath a park tree,
In a bed of fresh leaves,
A few moments with we entwind
"How Cool"
To slip into a "Dream"
With that thing you call just sport

(so sport the dance tween hawk and wolf) >>>

Barren Cliff of Chance

And so it came to pass one day …
Where one from barren cliff did dare
To upward gaze, and there, begin to stare,
In silent praise, the graceful flight
Of one who climbed the heights
To where but light of moon and star
Could touch its feathered outstretched wings.

Long and hard did come the howl
That strained to reach and touch
What then was but a dashing silhouette
Before a pair of eyes
That would not turn away and quit
Till came within the wind, its sweet decent
Upon a nearby branch to land and watch
What then became a circling, beckoning dance below …
Right there where one from barren cliff did dare to upward stare.

And so it came to pass
Where chirping flight and howling prance
Made chance a dance
Beneath that light of moon and star.
For although still afar
One Earth bound - One Sky Adrift
Did meet on barren cliff to sift
What just might come to last …
A Timeless Dance still bound to Circumstance.

And yet, like forsaken shattered bits of glass
That once held time now left in scattered sand
Beneath both glow of moon and shine of morning rise
Surprise!
Might heart and soul be so ~ and yet ~ I think it not
For such has life become ~ a gambit toss for gain.
And so, a bitter contemplate of who has upper hand
For shame!
The Dance on Barren Cliff left Undared

(before the crevice edge) >>>

The Crevice Edge

~~~~~~~~~~~~~~~~~~~~~~~~~~

At the crevice edge of heaving mountain peaks
I stand to take a peak to see if with but just one leap
I land within a pair of limbs,
Within a pair of open greeting arms to therein swim
Within a cool refreshing pond till
Roaring winds full of LOVE begin to blow again

Oh stirring joy that climbs beyond the here and now,
Now so full of frowns and sounds I wish would disappear
If only but for just a while to allow
This present call for wild
A wild within the drought of doubt filled clouds
Where my inner rain drops and thunder thoughts
Caught in need to be all poured OUT!

Set ablaze to scream new dreams to chase and taste
No more from crevice heaving mountain peaks
But valley streams of nerves below
Streams of tears tingling to run their course
Upon the fields of flesh made wet once touched

At crevice heaving mountain peaks where dared to feel that leap
Where open greeting arms do swim as one
Within a pond then shared to stir
The joys that climb beyond the here and now
To where within the glistening strands of hair to hold
A heat that simply cannot be compared

A flight from plight made so right – so deep in present light
To slowly grow within a pond that ever glows
And so
From crevice mountain peeks
To valley streams of roots below
I'm sold

(so do take flight) >>>

Take Flight

~~~~~~~~~~~~~~~~~~~~~~~~~~

And so I say take flight your feet
To bring your hands upon my doors to knock
Where then, once in to spend the night,
Embraced within each other's arms,
Flood gates unlocked to bring upon our flesh
The scented taste of sweat so sweet.
One dare not even contemplate
A pause to catch a breath or spare the heart from burst.

Take flight your feet
To meet and greet the fate of treats released to share
Once dared to go beyond these letter spotted sheets
And miles of copper wires strung between our ears.
Were we to stand before each others hands and eyes to greet,
To finger tingle tease both mind and soul,
To whisper words that start with please
Let not this moment pass.

Let our feet make haste to fly and try
The feast that now unfolds between our thoughts to hold
Until the cold of yesterday – Replaced!
By heat so strong to last all those days to come.
One thing be left to do
Take flight I say - make haste your feet
To bring your hands to knock upon my door
Where then, once in to spend the night
Embraced within each other's arms, a trick or two unfolds

(then side by side) >>>

Side by Side

Were it more than just wishful thoughts …
To roll my eyes and turn
The coming morning rise back into dark of night …
Where reawakened then there find
Each other smiling side by side.

Were the stretch of arm and hand
More than just an empty pillow touch …
A crown of golden strands to hold and smell,
A field of curves to gaze and roam upon with sweet caress,
A stream of warm and gentle breath like wind
To brush upon each others brow.

Were it more than just wishful thought
To firmly press against my chest
As if to make of two just one,
Each others inner voice released
Like waves upon each others shores made light
If but for just a while.

Then would a star light shine this night
To point and guide my dreams
As if to chart these present thoughts of unmet wants,
Where then to wake and find
Our smiling side by side fulfilled.

How then my fill of daily tasks
Be turned to acts of joy …
No longer bearing wishful thoughts outpoured
But vivid memories to chase and catch once more
Each other smiling side by side.

(and so do dare to want) >>>

29

I Want

I want to climb to heights
Where side by side
On a crescent moon and on a rising sun
Our sight to gaze upon.

I want to settle by a brook
Where we might share
The joyful sound of fresh new life
Begin to course our veins.

I want to count the stars
As if they were a sign
Of destined days where hand in hand
Our footprints in the sand we'd find.

And more
Like ocean waves that touch so many shores
While storing within its deep such wonders without end
I want to gaze upon your frame in sleep
And ponder what just might be within your dreams

To then
With gentle touch awake your smile,
An Invitation to embrace a set of dreams
In waves made real for us to often feel.

Where then
Your breath with mine in gasps
To break the silent still of sound
Replaced by sounds then made and claimed
Our Own

(within an outpoured heart) >>>

Outpoured Heart

If art opens the eye and words the mind,
What opens the heart to feel search and find
Tears that need to flow and faith that needs to grow
In truth right now, I do not know

I do not know
How down in deep
A two-edge sword does reach
To cut and tear asunder in both wonder and blunder …
At times to bleed a creed - At times to bleed a need
At times to bring the soul set free
Where then within the wind
Sometimes gentle, sometimes swift
Sometimes tempest storm it seems to be

Self! Made free from cling
To see how fears do begin to disappear
And thus, from rise to setting sun
The sum of inner void made clear
At times for cheer - At times for sneer.
EXTREMES they seem to be
The common cause to feel, search and find
The heart lay bare enough to cry
What depths both eye and mind can not

So tear out my eyes and still my mind
That I may always walk from deep inside
That I may always ride life's sword
And bleed the truth of all that be
That I may live from deep within
And swim love's river flowing to its end

Yes tear out my eyes and still my mind
For then I'll know I've lived to greet my end
Alive! With open heart - felt and found
A tearful flow of truth
And a faith that ever grows
To fly life's heights and depths
With a willing outpoured heart

(for another cry survived) >>>

Another Cry Survived

I wondered why to cry her eyes did grow
Until the hug that came
No doubt to soothe some innate pain
That came this day to rain on her parade

How so my want to reach and touch her soul
Where I might cause her inner light once more to glow
Amidst what cold and dark has come to quench her spark
Suffice be me to say fear not

Cry not without the thought
How liberating is the act
When from deep down one begins to feel
A cry in self still found

A heart that has not come to rot
A soul with dreams still found
A thought that questions why
So many fear the act of cry

Were I not placed so far in time and space
Were she not prone to others fly
Perhaps the nature that we share
Would dare our outstretched hands with much

And yet with just a bit of wine and dine
Beneath the twilight sky for us did shine
A common cause with which to thrive
… Another cry Survived …

(where agape love still does thrive) >>>

Agape Love

I've really not gone far but feel I best just stay away
Long enough to pray and pave the way
To where, though old and gray, we're meant to play
Where each other's hidden secrets lay
Where the tears of yesterdays on our todays
Are all just simply torn away

I'm not that far but feel I best just stay away
Long enough to pray and pave the way
To where our laugh and play still can
The twilight hours brave

In fact I'm not away just hid
Long enough to pray and pave the way
To where your face asleep I gaze upon and with a kiss
each other raised in whispered bliss

For moments where we in twilight walked
For moments where we laughed and talked
For moments where love steered the many pictures that we took
For moments where despair was left at mercy's brook
For moments where we laid and slept well embraced
For moments where with God well placed
Still, we, each other chased

So I've not gone long– just long enough to pray and pave the way
Not far – but feeling lonely and afraid
While looking for a way to say
I'm really here to stay – just not this way
Just not in strife-filled days
But with hope to cope and brave agape's love embraced

(be bound to a higher cause) >>>

Bound To Higher Cause

Were I not bound to higher cause
Your hand in mine at morning rise
And
On horizons new you by my side
Would surely be the prize.

Yet beyond all that could have been,
Beyond the fate our paths may never cross again,
Still stands the memory of how we danced
As the winds of chance did wrestle me to contemplate.
Were I not bound to higher cause
The flames of passion would have soared without discord.

So suffer not my eyes and ears with void
Just because we did not cross the line.
Suffer not tomorrow's doors with void
Just because we stand on different shores.
"Just simply try to rise."
For boundless reasons not yet clear
Don't simply fade and disappear.
For possibilities not yet seen do dare believe
"Nothing is simply just by chance."

For in my present state of mind
Where thought, like light of moon throughout the dark of night,
Like stars throughout the blanket sky, your shining eyes
Like endless waves upon the sea, your glistening smile
And though now bound by higher cause I be,
Upon horizons new the prize of you I see and want to seek

(So Dare) >>>

Dare

~~~~~~~~~~~~~~~~~~~~~~~~~~~~~~~~~~

When you hear me say
My place is in your inner space
"Please Dare Hold On"
To what I've got should you choose to stop
Let me try to make you purrrrrrrrrrrrrrrr
Like a cat just having found it's way to the Milky Way,
Let me rev you up like a wild mustang ready to cross the plains,
And like ice - cream melting at the touch of tongue
Still ready
To play and be molded like clay in the potters hand.
So Dare
Make yourself ready and simply pray
Cause coming your way
Like thundering rain clouds
To shower you with praise I am.
Dare
If you're quick and unafraid
Let me rain on your parade
Let me whisper in your ear
And like a deer at the alter ready to be carved
Watch how layer by layer the defenses disappear
Till everywhere
With a witty nip here and a tug of war there
The heated sounds of passion will begin to fill the air
If you're quick and unafraid
TO ALWAYS DARE …

(then accept love's compromise) >>>

A Morning Compromised

In the morning rise
Behind locked doors she sits
For what I do not know.
No doubt, like me, she's caught
In shattered dreams
Still close but compromised.

As the clock winds down
Time running out
Her inner silent shouts
No doubt still caught
In thoughts now fighting
Feelings, like those of a wounded beast.

So what now must I decide
With all that in me still resides
As she chooses to simply just withdraw
With shattered dreams of hope
Still close but compromised
For what I do not know

But dare I not fall into despair
Nor chance the thought of splitting hairs,
Dare I not to rights and wrongs compare
Nor press to change her present state.
For though not there right now
To break this present snare …
For this, uncompromised, I am indeed prepared

(with more than simple compromise) >>>

More Than Simple Compromise

I liked what I saw
Behind those big, dark, piercing
Bedroom eyes.
So much trapped deep down inside
Until at last
Your Longing, Wanting, and Waiting Cry
Unitl My my! Thought I!
No need to say good-bye
While into each other's arms we just might dive

And yet by chance, maybe choice
Both having run their course
Together we did not find
That special place beneath the twilight sky

Indeed it blows my mind

The thought of where you now preside,
The thought of who right now be by your side.
Were I to make rewind the time
No doubt I'd blow your mind.
I'd mend your heart and ring your chimes
I'd come and make you realize
That sometimes … there's more … much much more
than simple compromise

But will you call or stall
Will you even care at all
Will you mull it over
Or simply let it slip and fall
Upon deaf ears and blinded eyes.
Has all that could and would become undone
Suddenly Compromised?
Then do stop and ponder
There's really more than simple compromise

(so shhh and listen) >>>

SHHH

As I saw come out
From within the mist of my mental eye
In full, firm force and stride
You! Passionate, Exciting and Enticing …
Motioning and Compelling … Me!

Open hearted – Open Armed
Charmed with Anticipation
Making wild and active my imagination
While awakened to discovered somewhere deep
Emotion and Affection,
An Infatuation where
You … Me … We
Found in a sudden contemplation
SHHH

(to flow glow and grow) >>>

We Flow! Glow! Grow!

~~~~~~~~~~~~~~~~~~~~~~~~~~~~~~~~~~~~~~~

We flow! We glow! We grow!
Our smiles guiding us to a time and place
That makes all else wait,
A time in space that makes all else erased!

As our moves elate and elude
We put ourselves in a mood able to see
Where Jupiter and Mars don't collide but align
Spirit, Soul and Mind.

Now we! Heavenly bodies suddenly entwined
In a stable full of moves that groove,
Full of moody moments within the twilight zone
Where just beyond its thunder dome we're suddenly home

Home! Where moans and groans are but our dreams made manifest
Home! Where things are made tried and true
Because we flow! Because we glow!
Because we move to trace the skies
Till the stars form images to contemplate
The flow that flows glows and grows

(sometimes becoming an obsession) >>>

Obsession

~~~~~~~~~~~~~~~~~~~~~~~~~~~~~~~~~~~~~~~

All in one – Everything wrong - Everything right
With all might, regardless of what price in strife,
Clung and held so tight – An obsession throughout the night
To run or fight … to cry, to pray, to sigh … I can't decide

Cause without commotion - In motion
Suddenly encased in lace
Suddenly embraced in wait
An endless field of dreams to chase

A morning rising sun
While heart beats raging like a drum
A bead of sweat that clings to brow
As a distant melody from soul well sung begins to form

And so with all my might – regardless of what price in strife
Clung and held so tight – this obsession in the night
While to cry, to pray, to sigh, to run or fight … I can't decide
All in one, all alone, all in whisper while all nearly made undone

Can you sense and hear the "dear"?
The "dear" that says come here?
The "dear" that says come near?
The "dear" that fights the fear?

Can you bring what's yet to come
Can you bring from there a song
Can you bring from there a swing
Can you bring from grief to life that age long feeling for a fling

Cause while to cry, to pray, to sigh, to run or fight one can't decide
Clung to tight – this obsession throughout the night
And with all my might – regardless what price in strife
Of this obsession dare I say … A moment still not done!

(but in wait to wake and roll) >>>

A Mornings Wake and Roll

I woke and rolled this morning
Wishing to have found you sleeping by my side.
The thought of my touch making you roll your eyes with sigh
Releasing wanting joy from deep inside
Where surely I'd match your swaying hips with mine

If only for a moment come your lips
To cross and brush with mine
Then surely we would climb the heights and find
Our names inscribed
Upon the clouds with every morning rise

Might I surmise this thought
Be found and shared with you to dare,
To lend a hand that says
Indeed! let be our need confessed
To find ourselves entwined

Our flesh in pleasure sweat
Embraced to chase away the cold and lonely nights
Where then our days be filled with bliss filled thoughts
And a love filled kiss that says
Our fate is signed and sealed

To wake and roll the morning rise
And find our sleeping side by side
Where with rolling eyes and sighs
Our wanting joy from deep inside released
By having matched our swaying hips
In a morning wake and roll

(that ends with a twilight thought) >>>

Sleep Tight

Sleep tight within my arms
And feel the daily storms subside.
Let not tomorrows deeds surpass
This moment's quest to last

For never has it been
Nor ever shall it be again …
This first between us dared and shared,
This moment now beyond compare

Our stares into each other's eyes
As if to seek and touch the soul,
As if our hair within each other's hands,
As if to make this moment ever stand

Against the tempest rage
That comes to fill the thought with doubt …
Against the desert heat
That comes to wither all that seeks to grow

And so I say sleep tight within my arms this night
To feel the daily storms subside.
For though tomorrows deeds may come to press against our wants
This moments quest has come to stand the test of time

(where then I do dare pray) >>>

Pray

She was and is
Strong, Beautiful and full of charm
But I was wrong
To think it could last long
The song that hides the strife she bore
For so, so long

She was and is strong
A beauty full of so much to discover and explore
But I was wrong
To think I could defuse and not loose
Against her scattered bombs waiting to go off
For so, so long

She was and is strong beautiful and full of charm
But I was wrong – believing that no harm would come,
Wrong to survive her constant barrage and somehow hold on,
Wrong to have stood before her knife of sudden strife
For now I stand battle torn and all alone

And yet I can't forget!
Amidst all the frets of despair and regret
The love God gave to live in me for her …
A love that braves enough to play
A love still willing to pay and not stray
A love for those still able to pray

(and so I do lament) >>>

Lament

I lament death's scent
On a love that once came and now has went

Bent and brought down low
Before loves alter I lament
The dark caverns full of rotted roots beneath
Where once did come a love that came and now has gone

I lament – bent and spent
With no place to repent,
With no one for fun beneath the sun,
With no "say cheese" for the camera shots to keep,
No breeze of please to bring about appease

I lament – bent and spent, a vacant space for rent,
A space now laced with memories no longer chased,
A space where once the race was almost won,
A space now used to deposit waste
Because erased! A love that once came and now has gone
And so for a love that came and went – I lament

(love's gone) >>>

Love Gone

Last night I watched a sunset
And damn!
This morning I watched a sunrise
And damn!
But just now I watched a movie
And do conclude

Love! Unmet not lost
Just Gone! To the seabed of broken trust
Where then

I dreamed and remembered
How I said, you to me, God gave
How I said, life without you, I can't
And yet, now learn I must

Love! Unmet not lost
Just Gone! To the seabed of broken trust
Where once

I held you! I embraced you! I caressed you!
And even though now distanced – its you I still long to hold
Till the fading of last hopes came and went
Where now learn I must

Love! Unmet not lost
Just Gone! To the seabed of broken trust

(a sad and empty space) >>>

Sad & Empty Space

How sad and empty now it seems …
This space so suddenly made incomplete
Beneath the satin sheets.
Were things tween us not so distantly discrete
Embraced we'd fall asleep
And on horizons new we'd greet …
A candle lit well-cooked meal
Where then beneath the stellar twilight sheets
As one we'd walk the streets
Exchanging tricks and treats
Where then dispelled! This sad and empty feel
By dreams rekindled and made real once more.
And with hearts no longer made of steel
With words that say "New Deal"
Once more beneath the satin sheets
Rekindled and made complete
Embraced we'd gently fall asleep
In spite of all lifes
Tricks & Treats
That seek to make our time a sad and empty space

(cause I still remember) >>>

Parting Sway

Our eyes and paths did cross
Distantly once or twice till then ...
When face to face, a smile
And thoughts set out to break the ice.

Who I asked
And "a fleeting friend" said you
I asked again
And "ME is Me" said you
Where then you turned and swayed away
Leaving me dismayed.

Now contemplating and amazed ...
Your smile, your face, your frame ...
Your legs, your arms, your hands ...
Your skin so soft, so tight and fair ...
Your hair, long dark strands full of waves...
A package laced in pride and grace to see.

And so to memory, you I did well place
Till crossed our eyes and path once more
'Till face to face, another smile exchanged
With thoughts once more embraced
Before we part once more as friends

(Home) >>>

Home

~~~~~~~~~~~~~~~~~~~~~~~~~~~~~~~~~~~

And so I wish I could
Discretely give into this breeze
That comes to cool
The heat I just can't seem to dissipate.
I wish I could
Just simply close my eyes and wait
For fate to come and wash it all away;
All that's been now here inscribed
Upon my present slate to bear.
I wish I could
Dare brave this sense
Of being no more than but love's slave
Long enough to weather out
The pain that right now stains my soul.
Though home, for the moment, be a heated battle ground
Home is where I need and want to go.
Home is where I know
My heart will find its resting place.
So why procrastinate these first few steps?
When there is no better place than home
Home!
That place where peace for us does wait

(a second chance) >>>

Still Does Wait

Beneath the façade of all you now portray,
Beneath all that you keep at bay,
Lonely, empty, and afraid …
Alas! You stand betrayed.

Before the mirror of truth and light,
Torn by strife you stand
In search to find at your command
That which would not be compromised,
That which would surpass all your years now past.
So to make your present waves
A warm and gentle thing to sum your worth
Do fight to chase your fear of coming days away.

Oh that you would take my hand
And for a breath or two let me in you reside.
To make life's ride mean more than simple compromise
Arise to watch the coming sun
while we still standing side by side.

For beneath the façade of all you now portray,
Beneath all that you keep at bay,
I see in you a thing that still remains …
A thing not yet unleashed,
A thing that will not cease
Until true inner peace you find.
And so like morning dew upon a mountain peak
Still Does Wait
Our soul refreshed to carry on
Still Does Wait
Our soul refreshed to carry on

(where then there again) >>>

Pulling Back The Sheets

Once more
I've searched for you within my sleep
and with the morning rise
With outstretched open arms
I've pulled the blankets back
Where nothing have I found.

Long and gray shall this day be
Without your smiling frame to see and feel.
Once more too far from me you are

But if by chance somewhere out there
You've dared a thought of me
Then once again this night I'll brave
'Till morning light with outstretched hands in faith
Once more the blanket sheets I'll pull.

For as never has the rooster
Ceased his morning cry
Or the wolf
His evening howl
Never shall this desire come to die
You need not wonder why

(that silent moment) >>>

That Silent Moment

Within that silent moment
I said
Give me your body and I shall give the world my soul
But in truth my heart would remain true with but just you

I said
Give me the gasping breaths of your passion
And like smoke rising to the heavens
I'd inscribe prayers for the human race
But in truth for two paths made one I'd bow

For when I said
Let my fingers form ripples upon your flesh
And you shall see your inner thoughts made real
I meant look into my eyes and see our wishing well unfold

And when I said that
If by chance the flood gates of your eve should burst
You'll see an ark upon its waves joining forces tween you and me
I meant endless as the ocean be our story yet to tell

For it would be our inner ears
Made weary and deaf by the mundane
That I'd seek to rekindled with newfound hope
And to our own joy add days unbound

Need more be said of that silent moment
When first your shoulders in my hands made bare,
When first I caressed them with my lips
As my gaze the rest of you I traced

And as my breath dared become a gasp
As my thoughts raced to beg you not to leave
In subtle silence I withdrew
Hoping that this silent moment
Was felt by you as well

(and so I said) >>>

Give me your heart

Give me your heart
To start your pulse anew
And like the stars that spark the dark of night
With light suffice to chart a path from here to there
I'd dare make your stare a thing to last within a dance

Give me your soul
To mold your course anew
And like the wind that moves the clouds
With gentle shoves suffice to turn them inside out
I'd dare make your every wish come true

Give me your dreams
To start your screams anew
And like ice cream melting in my hands
With taste suffice to bring about a lick or two
I'd dare make your breath like wind flowing through life's trees

For then your flesh
To bring within my gaze and grasp
Like silhouettes upon horizons new we'd dance
And with sweet sweat rhythms then released
I'd dare embrace your inner warmth unleashed

(because I hold you deep in heart) >>>

Place In My Heart

There is a place within my heart ... so vast it seems
Constantly calling out to me.
Sometimes I hear ... sometimes it's not clear
A wordless something that sounds like ... Here! I'm here

Deep longing stirs in me ... so vast it seems
Endlessly pulling at me
Sometimes I adhere ... sometimes it's simply just not clear
A shapeless somewhere that feels like ... There! I'm there

I fight to listen and understand ... so vast it seems
I strain to see and comprehend
Sometimes I ache ... sometimes I'm empty and unclear
Making pools of tears well up with emotions like ... I love, and I fear

It's then, in that moment, for but only that seemingly endless moment
Like comets with their fiery trails streaking across the sky
Scorching the very nature of my souls eye
Suddenly! I, small and remorse filled, begin to ache, hear and adhere

"I am" it says ... always was and will be
Infinite with the infinite ... ever flowing ... ever evolving
Toward that which was and is meant to be ... ME!
Still wild but not yet free I wonder ... who is me?

Unsettled and shaken onto bended knees ... my head to humble bow it falls
I still know not to what, why or how
But that which is not yet ... is already set
And so, to my own undoing, I fret

Because that's it ... I am ... still not yet all that will be
With not yet all that is to hear or see
And yet, endowed with possibility
I simply sit deep down within tranquility
To let it all just simply be, deep down within unknown tranquility,
LET'S ALL BE STILL

Still within that inner place of heart
Constantly calling out

(in such a twisted way) >>>

53

Twisted

Twisting my present sight
With things I thought long gone,
With things still yet to come,
Twisted now my mind I find.

She came and went as if a blast of wind
That turned me round and inside out!
How could this be so wrong
Yet feel so right on time?

With but one night full of words, drinks, and dance,
With just your shinning hair and deep dark eyes,
Some window pain in me got smashed
And sparked a different way to see
This twisted thing ain't just by chance!
And so, with just a one-night stand, I simply can't!

So Wham! Bam! No Thank You Ma'am!
Cause with everything and everyone
Now completely out of sight and mind …
You're right!
Perhaps I need to breathe fresh air,
Perhaps I need to brush my hair,
Perhaps I need to stop and contemplate.
So "INDEED" Let's Now Begin To Dance!
Let's now just begin to ask

What is this thing we right now share?
Where can this begin to go?
Why should we refrain in fear?
Who said it only sparks in fairy tales?
When will we take flight and see
When "HOW" is all we need for "NOW" …
How to match each others stare …
How to match each other's steps …
Cause Right Here And Now … Dumbfounded! I do stand
Dumbfounded by your blinding flash of light,
By your dare for me to brave,
By what might be – were we to ride these present waves
… **TWISTED** … Across the open seas of life

(oh if only I could paint) >>>

If I could paint

If I could paint
I'd capture the sunrays streaking through my windowpane
Racing in to brush my face with warmth suffice to cause a smile.
If I could paint
I'd capture the wind creaking through the cracks
The rain drops slowly pressing up against the glass
The magic rhythms only nature could create,
While for your embrace once again I'd wait.
If I could paint
I'd paint you standing by my side
I'd paint your charismatic sway released,
Unleashed to captivate my sense of sight, smell, and sound …
My longing sense to taste all that you just might be …
A pearl right before my eyes to gaze upon
Where then, like ocean waves that seems to have no end
I would indeed transcend
Your wildest dreams and screams.
If and only if I could
I'd paint you as a rainbow
Stretched across sky's span of space and time
Where then, I'd worry not this fleeting image in my mind.
I'd simply wait and watch
Your endless trail of flames
Get painted on the eternal canvas of my soul

(just to blow my mind) >>>

A Blowing of the Mind

It blows my mind each and every time
I see you passing by …
Your eyes, your smile and swaying stride
That makes me want to say please stay …
Let's play a game in life
Far from common fight and strife
Each and every time
We meet and greet for another dance with chance.
So
Let's just simply, simply
Blow each other's mind

(with maracas in the night) >>>

Maracas in the night

Like a well-tuned clock your name
Ticks through the corridors of my mind.
Like an endless, timeless, rhythmic dance
That guides my feet with precise beats it is.

It races through my brain like a priceless chain of pearls
Reflecting precious memories that always make me smile.
It fills my heart with loves passion rekindled hot,
It tingles my fingers with a need to reach and touch,
It fills my arms with desires to hold you firm
And as my loins do fill with unquenched yearn
A kindred story still waiting to unfold.

My ears burn with the echoes of your voice
My lips vibrate and pucker up without choice
My eyes seek your image in the skies
As you sparkle my nights and shine my days

And so here lies my silent fight and fright …
As my nerves rattle to rock you like maracas thru the night
As my stomach churns to pound you like a water drum
As my breath begins to heave a trumpet tune for you to keep
As my soul seeks hope close and deep … there is you!
For without you there will be no pulse, no life or prize.
There is no pulse, no life, or prize
Without you to rock like maracas thru the night

(cause you are my chispa/sparks) >>>

La Chispa/Spark

Outstanding!
La chispa/spark has done done it again!
Like a sudden rush of swirling wind
She's done spun and turned me inside out
In ways where now … Exposed!
Exposed! All I am and can come to feel!
Exposed! All my thoughts and dreams revealed!
Exposed! My love to dance, hike, and bike
Exposed! Poetic notes tween us exchanged
Filling a book for all to someday see …
To see that yes indeed! Fairy tales do come to sometimes be
Cause La Chispa/spark has done done it again.
She's pressed my brain to hear her words
Pressed my eyes to keep her frame within my gaze …
Amazed! By desires to have her walking by my side
Amazed! By desires to shower her with praise
And so I Growl! "It's On!"
Till well past dawn and into yet another setting sun
I Growl! "It's On!"
Till one beneath the blanket of stars above we are
And all else be made gone
Gone
With the Chicago Blues and a Georgia song to carry on
Cause La Chispa/spark is simply just right on
She's on a mission all her own
And though soul mates do not possess
They do caress both mind and flesh,
They do transcend common boundary lines.

And so!
Because we're destined to sometimes parallel and share.
I say "Who cares"
With you and me upon the wings of wind
Competing to complete the ride un-compromised
I know … for us … A prize does wait

(Because you are my Nubien Queen)

A Nubian Queen with some old school R&B

To my Nubian Queen i tip my head with hat in hand
In wait to catch a drop or two right from her heart
As if from windows to her soul
Where that secret place in her I want to touch so tenderly.
Yes! So tenderly I'd like to touch her long enough to make her stick around awhile
Long enough to share a chat and some good old school R&B.
YES to my Nubian Queen I tip my head with hat in hand
In want to catch her eye and hold her hand in mine
Where then I'd dare not look away much less even think of letting go …
Her gaze, her hand, her heart and soul
A treasure chest full of stuff for me to hold
Her frame within my arms, her waist and back within a dance
Where she, her curves like ocean waves for me to ride out to horizons new
Where sun – rise or set made one as if perhaps we can also be …
Two fishes in the sea, two stallions runnin across the desert sands
Two turtle doves tumbling in the sky, two jungle bunnies
Jumping to the throbbing heart of tribal drums where with spirits then released
We unleashed to claim both stars and moon as crowns upon our brow.
Oh yea! Were she to look n see as me
A we that can then play hide n seek, trick n treat, monkey see n monkey do
Like captain kangaroo – me n her and her n me
Hopping with hope, jumping thru the ropes of fate while slipping into darkness
Where with eyes closed n minds relaxed we find each other in a dream
Just waiting to wake up as we
Me with tilted head n hat in hand
Her that Nubian Queen before my eyes to ever greet
With some good old school R&B …
A ripened treat made just right for
Me and my Nubian Queen
(upon a field of orange rays) >>>

Fields of Orange Rays

On fields beneath the Orange Rays of setting sun
Desires cup we filled to brim
With fresh crushed grapes to share.
Had it not been but our first
On the open plains
These rays we would have dared horizons new.
Cause In endless, seamless flow,
Like ocean waves beneath moons glow
I'd move your innermost
'Tween yellow brights and fire reds
Just to hear you roar,
Just to watch you claw your way
Toward heights that only eagles brave
Where then! No Doubt! We'd be on our way

With desires cup filled to brim
And the orange rays we dared,
With the purple grapes we shared
And the thoughts we plowed,
Love's seeds we'd place with care
Beneath these field of orange rays
Where Passions Depths We'd then dare Brave.

So hear my whispers in your ears,
Feel breath begin to trace our skin
And sense our hearts begin to race
As my fingers brush your sides
Just to have you sigh from deep inside.
So hear the whispers in our minds
And feel the ripples beneath our skin,
See the exploration in our eyes
And brave the flow with dare.
Can you hear winds whisper in the air
And feel its chill tightening up our limbs?
Can you sense raindrops forming in the soul
And dare prolong the growing thirst to quench?
Then leave behind all sense of time,
All sense of fear and pain,
All sense of guilt and shame.
For now … Beneath these Orange Rays of Bliss
Its time to Give and Take it all in stride.

(just because its time) >>>

Time

The times have come and gone
To where so much but us has come to rest
Like memories of days and nights
Full of people, places, and things now no more
Yet, here we are

Old and grey but standing strong
Because we found our own love song to carry on.
To mark each year with faith filled gifts of praise
And so! For all we've stayed beneath Gods grace
Here we are

Shooting stars across a sky so full of times now come and gone …
Our light still burning bright - untouched by strife or fight
Because we found within our hearts – our own love song.
Because we found a greater cause full of endless reasons to hold on
Here we are

Still encased in love's embrace
Still compelled by dreams to chase
Still opening doors where more awaits
Where nothing says to us too late
Just because … Here we are

Amidst the signs of times now come and gone
Amidst so much being put to rest
Having stood the test of time – still willing to struggle seek and find
Memories of days and nights to fill with love and life
Here we are! Still blessed with time to blow each other's mind

(Its time to admit)

Everlasting Treasure

~~~~~~~~~~~~~~~~~~~~~~~~~

A lifelong everlasting treasure chest is she
A companion through life's storms she's always been
An unconditional, faithful love till end in her I find
A friendship that just won't bend or rend
For nothing less than her best she brings
As if she has no end or needs to pass

A lifelong everlasting treasured gem is she
Without regret, beyond life's strife and grief, she does ascend
Without limit, beyond conviction and belief, she does transcend
And though come life's pain she somehow still remains the same
For In blind faith, somehow, her heart and soul she does defend

A lifelong everlasting treasured gem is she
No crown of king has ever seen her glow
No thought to comprehend has forth been sought
No words in book or speech has yet been wrought
And though my heart may come and go – songs for her I hold
For truly has she ever been – an everlasting, treasured gem

(a cloud to rest upon) >>>>

A cloud to rest ones head

Surrounded by the glow of scented candles
And passion sounds that touch …
Memories do take hold
And thoughts of you are sparked.
A fragrant taste of chilled crushed grapes,
A hand to reach and draw you near
And then, with swaying hips in warm embrace,
Our eyes and lips do engage ...
To journey where only loving trust can fly,
To find that place where dreams come true,
To where fear is made to disappear
And pain is made but pulse that says
"Alive to feel love's come and go"
Now love's inner voice does wait
A chance to say I'm here!
Beyond the threat of time and space
To make exchanged like breath,
Like precious gems upon a royal crown
While dancing 'tween life's many rows of thorns,
Thorns that say a rose to pluck is near.
Oh that you would dare to brave
Tomorrow free of past
Long enough to plant
Those seeds that in deep sleep
'Till shine of summer sun does say,
Regardless of the winter frost … Arise!
A blossomed unique thing now seen,
God's grace for you and I arrived,
Victory's flag upon life's battlefield,
Upheld for all to see.
Indeed the road of blood stained sweat
Does yield a promise still.
For the fearless brows of those that dare
To chance on nothing less
Than love's gentle cloud to rest one's head

(because she's been and is) >>>

You've Been And Is

~~~~~~~~~~~~~~~~~~~~~~~~~~~~~~~~~~~~

Through out the many years now come and gone
You've been … You is.
Through my child like walks and adolescent talks,
Through my adult strides onto these times so full of gray
You've been … You is
A beacon shining bright with rays of love and hope to cope
A bridge between what was and is
to safely cross the many storms untouched
That you've been and more

My evening star that smiles
Even from afar
The gentle breeze that fills my sails with joy
And carries me onto horizons new
Every time that comes to me the thought of you
So tall and strong your faith
So full of grace your face
Suffice to keep my heart and soul with God in place

To chase and taste along the path of life
Many memories still alive
Many seasons yet to arrive
So many reasons to survive
Because you've been and is
With every morning rise
A special part of me uncompromised
Because you've always been and always is
My evening shining star

(your fire joy and electric lights) >>>

Fire, joy and electric lights

With a smile that can shine
Through the darkest cloud
I do dare say
With but just one look
your sparking eyes … suffice to testify
You're a Latin delight, feisty and full of fight!
Able to climb the heights
And make everything alright
Cause I tell you no lie
You're fire, joy and electric lights.
From the strands of your long dark hair
To the very tips of your shiny toes
It's easy to tell - You wild
Wild and able to cast spells.
With but just the touch of your hand
You entice my chance to strongly glance
At your rock solid stance …
Able to put me into a trance to chance
Me rocking in my pants
With but just one dance.
Cause I tell you no lie
You're fire, joy, and electric lights
A voice that can thunder
Deep down in my soul
An attempt to ascend and transcend
Beyond the pretend
Just to make you my friend
Cause you're fire, joy, and electric lights

(but does she know it) >>>

Does she know?

Does she know?
What if she did – what then would …
Beneath moons glow and sunrise shine
Would heart and mind as one be made,
Would side by side hand in hand be seen?
Does she know?
What if she did – what then would …
Within Gods watch … His guide
Would friendship rise and trust be forged,
Would blessings be unbound?
Does she know?
What if she did – what then would …
What would one, could one, should one do?
Let not come waist thru haste …
Best give time and space its dew …
Cause she just might come to know!
And so
"What if" can then become "What is"
When she finally comes to know!

(because she's gold) >>>

She's Gold

She's always treated me like gold
Though through the years I do come and go
Though off and on I'm cold
No matter what – She's always treated me like gold
And so I'm sold – she's much, much more than gold

She's a royal bloodline from a loyal place and time
She knows my every dream – in peace I sleep with her by my side
She knows my every line – fearlessly I live with her inside
She's one of a kind – and to God in thanks I pray – she mine
And so I'm sold – she's much, more than gold

With her embrace so warm, gentle, and kind
I climb the heights and dare beyond my place and time
With her embrace so unconditional and unreserved
I'll brave my ship against the current trend
And so I'm sold – she's much, more than gold

She's where I always run to hide and heal
She's where I always go to show and tell
She's where I'll always find my human heart revealed
She's where my last breath I will unveil
And so I'm sold – she much, much more than gold

So, if ever another fight for me to brave
If ever another mark for me to chase
If come another defeat for me to face
No matter how old or cold I be – Let it be her embrace I find
Because I'm sold – she's much, much more than gold

(regardless of all the twist and turns we take) >>>

Our crooked path that doesn't seem to dim

Forget the he and she – forget the you and me –
forget the differences tween our time and space
We're here and always been right from the very start
We've been in and out each other's path without a glitch
We've freely come and gone and still hold on
Cause from where we met till now
Partners in crime we've somehow been
Already seen! The northern lights in each other's eyes
Already climbed the mountain top
and seen the glory in each other's smile
We've already crossed the waters tween our shores
And with unspoken words
we've touched each other's hearts
As longing brushes our soul in ways only God can tell
Need we embrace or kiss to sense the path ahead
Need we refrain from embarking the journey still "yets to come"
Need we abide by the boundaries standing tween "what might"
When heart knows not such things
Let Attraction become infatuation – Let love make one of two
has not such thoughts tip toed through our contemplations
Then let's ride adventures waves
and let the cards fall where they may
Let destiny pave the way - let it have final say
Lets no longer walk on eggs
Lets satisfy the secret hunger we've dared not entertain
Let come and go the quarrels we've survived
Let friendships healing force always bring resolve
cause from the start to here –perhaps we'll always be
A crooked path that doesn't seem to dim

(because love does not end – it transcends) >>>>

Love Transcends

Once more! Unexpected and unanticipated
Come, in the twilight hours of the night
In solid shape and form - a vivid dream damn near screamed
Where me - felled before the forbidden wishing well

We didn't really look or speak - even a handshake was far from reach
But amidst light words and lingering thoughts exchanged!
Amidst a moments slip - uncovered - A lovers prayer!
Where me - felled before the forbidden wishing well

Amidst the silence and quick glances shared
I woke with a painful sting made real
A need to rise and pace – A need to wash my face
A need to trace in words – this sudden need to yell

Once more – let the taunting torment die
And like a raven with shining outstretched wings,
Its screaming leap into swift flight through the wind
Once more I echoed Yea – Come Love's Double Sided Blade

And like a finger pricked by a rose's thorn
From my heart now caught – an echoed yea escapes
A yea that says indeed "Love Does Not End But Transcends"
It ascends to heights of heart and mind
It descends to depths of flesh and bone
While once more me at the forbidden wishing well
Once more to Realize: Love Does Not End But Transcends

Pretty Pink

Oh pretty pink
Whose wink does catch my eye,
Whose veils do flap like flags before a royal gate
Where so much more does wait.
Oh pretty pink
Whose glistening path engulfs me deep in sighs
Where, while feeling your velvet soft,
Your joy unleashed once reached and touched
Oh pretty pink
How I wish you'd simply just believe
All you are and more …
A gentle place so full of peace.
A sign of what the world could be,
If you'd simply just believe
All the things I say and see …
Your mind that probes with such delight,
Your ways that spark such thought
For those who take the time
To graze along your side
And hear your inner sighs revealed.
Oh pretty pink
Might I prevail to dry your eyes
Each time you come to cry.
Might I prevail to mirror true
An image to simply just believe
All you are and more … Yes all you are and more
In ways that dare the ride,
The waves of life somewhere beyond …
Beyond the weight of all one comes to bare,
Beyond the passing hurts and fears,
Beyond desires to offend
Where then, able to transcend …
Able to Transform …
Able to Evolve …
Your pretty pink revealed

(and for my granddaughter Claudia – aka - Rugrat) >>>

Rugrat

~~~~~~~~~~~~~~~~~~~~~~~~~~~~~~~~~

As seeds to fertile ground in mama's womb you fell
And in its silent dark you churned and churned
Till with boom n bang – time did set you free
… A summer sprout to blossom bloom …
And blossom bloom you did!
Through seasons on and on that came
Sometimes warm to hot …
Sometimes cool to cold …
No matter what you grew …
More so … you blossom bloomed
Shedding your youthful skin in stages
As you fought to claim and forge a path all your own.
And so you did – and so you have
And so I know you ever will
As I so proudly watched and no doubt always will.
For though you now in womanhood
on and on you'll move
My Little Rugrat that you'll always be … yes …
No matter what
My Little Rugrat - that you'll always be
Happy Birthday
4/2020

Closing Thoughts

From the start **I contemplated** what documenting my journey through love's ups and downs would look like in a series of poems. **I revisited** many of the people, places and times now long gone. And I must say, strolling through memory lane became surprisingly vivid and alluring. Many of them drew blood from my heart's present state of mind with deepened sensations. **Sensations** like sorrow, regret, joy, appreciation, excitement, fear, and yes love, were all made one in an emotional ball of jelly. To it all, I tipped my hat and said "OK"! Pick a bunch from the many and let the reader sense, experience, and relate. I hope I made the right choices.

I usually worked these poems with wordless jazz music in the background and floated through the clouds of memories to imagine future possibilities. I rode the waves of inspiration to **uncharted shores** within my heart. Sometimes I got so deep that I, in one thoughtful image, got lost in time and space. Nothing else but the moment existed. I loved it! If but for a moment in time, I loved the art of loving! Physically, mentally, emotionally and spiritually! They all count as special moments to explore. Perhaps these works will trigger couples to share, even recite to each other.

Like right now! I just stumbled into a sexy set of poems that triggered the memory of someone I have not connected with in more than a year. Interesting how the spark was strong enough to make me recite as if she were here to woo once more. More interesting when you, the reader, stumble into a poem that triggers your own sparks to wrestle with.

So strange how at times I press the keyboard as if it were a piano. Other times I press the keys as if I were striking a punching bag. Sometimes I stare into the screen as if it were a portal for time travel. Combined with background music, one word, one thought, spun me into oblivion. Lost in time and space until … suddenly … I come up for air to once more brave the task at hand: To labor through the collection of poems in order to place you on **an emotional roller coaster** able to take you into your own abyss.

<u>Available for live recitals</u>

For samplers see my video collection
On You Tube
Jose Yrizarry
347-865-3160
<u>Joepy4@yahoo.com</u>

Printed in the United States
by Baker & Taylor Publisher Services